Alpha

Published by Alpha International, HTB Brompton Road, London SW7 1JA.
Email: internationalpublishing@alpha.org
Website: alpha.org
@alphacourse

Contents

WELCOME TO ALPHA – A SERIES OF INTERACTIVE SESSIONS TO DISCUSS LIFE AND THE CHRISTIAN FAITH IN AN INFORMAL, FUN AND FRIENDLY ENVIRONMENT.

This guide outlines the content of the fifteen talks, which each look at a different aspect of the Christian faith. After each talk, there is a time for discussion in small groups – a place where you can ask questions, delve into different issues and find out what others think.

This is your guide, so use it however you like. Write, scribble, note, jot or doodle. Whatever helps.

My notes:

Session 1

Is there
more to
life
than this

Alpha

What, if any, has been your experience of Christianity?
- **Boring?**
- **Untrue?**
- **Irrelevant?**

At the heart of the Christian faith is a person: Jesus Christ. **Jesus said, 'I am the bread of life.' (John 6:35)**

1. JESUS SAID, 'I AM THE WAY.'

The first-order questions of life:
- Is there more to life than this?
- What am I doing on earth?
- What is the point of life?
- What is the purpose of my life?
- Where am I heading?

C. S. Lewis: 'I believe in Christianity as I believe that the sun has risen: not only because I see it, but because by it I see everything else.'[1]

Jesus is the lens through which we see God. He is the way to God.

Jesus is also the lens by which we see the world in a totally different dimension and clarity.

2. JESUS SAID, 'I AM THE TRUTH.'

C. S. Lewis: 'Christianity, if false, is of no importance, and if true, of infinite importance. The only thing it cannot be is moderately important.'[2]

- Truth – understood intellectually (head knowledge)
- Truth – experienced as a relationship (heart knowledge)

3. JESUS SAID, 'I AM THE LIFE.'

'I have come that [you] may have life, and have it to the full' (John 10:10).

Jesus came to deal with:
- The things that spoil our lives
- Our guilt

God loves you and he came, in the person of his Son, Jesus, to set you free to enjoy life to the full.

Jesus said, 'I am the way and the truth and the life'

(JOHN 14:6)

RECOMMENDED READING

What's So Amazing About Grace?
Philip Yancey

Why Jesus?
Nicky Gumbel

Session 2

Who is
Jesus

Alpha

Did Jesus exist?
- Evidence outside the New Testament about Jesus includes:
  - Tacitus and Suetonius, Roman historians
  - Josephus, Jewish historian
- Evidence within the New Testament

How do we know that what was written down in the New Testament has not been changed over the years?

ANCIENT WRITINGS

Key

Time lapse ▬▬▬▬▬▬▬ = 200 years   ● Number of copies found

Original work first written

30–310 years

NEW TESTAMENT

Copies found:

5,000+ Greek

10,000 Latin

9,300 Other languages

WORK	WHEN WRITTEN	EARLIEST COPY	TIME LAPSE	COPIES
HERODOTUS	488–428 BC	AD 900	1,300 years	8
THUCYDIDES	c. 460–400 BC	c. AD 900	1,300 years	8
TACITUS	AD 100	AD 1100	1,000 years	20
CAESAR'S *GALLIC WAR*	58–50 BC	AD 900	950 years	9–10
LIVY'S *ROMAN HISTORY*	59 BC – AD 17	AD 900	900 years	20
NEW TESTAMENT	AD 40–100	AD 130 (full manuscripts AD 350)	30–310 years	5,000+ Greek 10,000 Latin 9,300 others

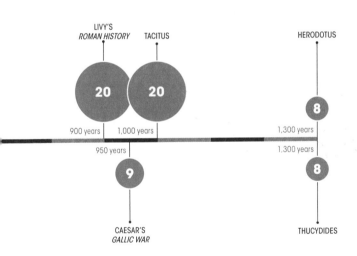

Was Jesus fully human?

- He had a human body
  - Tired (John 4:6)
  - Hungry (Matthew 4:2)

- He had human emotions
  - Anger (Mark 11:15–17)
  - Love (Mark 10:21)
  - Sadness (John 11:32–36)

- He had human experiences
  - Temptation (Mark 1:13)
  - Learning (Luke 2:46–52)
  - Work (Mark 6:3)
  - Obedience (Luke 2:51)

Was he more than a man, a great human, a religious teacher?
(Matthew 16:13–16)

1. WHAT DID HE SAY ABOUT HIMSELF?

- Teaching centred on himself
  - 'I am the bread of life' (John 6:35)
  - 'If the Son sets you free, you really will be free.' (John 8:36, NLT)
  - 'I am the light of the world' (John 8:12)
  - 'I am the way and the truth and the life' (John 14:6)
  - 'Come to me...' (Matthew 11:28–29)
  - Receive me – receive God (Matthew 10:40)
  - Welcome me – welcome God (Mark 9:37)
  - If you have seen me you have seen God (John 14:9)

- His indirect claims
  - To forgive sins (Mark 2:5)
  - To judge the world (Matthew 25:31,32,40,45)

- His direct claims
  - Messiah (Mark 14:61–62)
  - Son of God (Mark 14:61)
  - God the Son (John 20:26–29)
  - 'I and the Father are one.' (John 10:30)

Author of *The Chronicles of Narnia* and Oxford historian
C. S. Lewis wrote:

> 'A man who was merely a man and
> said the sort of things Jesus said would
> not be a great moral teacher. He would
> either be [insane]... or else he would be
> "the Devil of Hell". You must make your
> choice. Either this man was, and is, the
> Son of God, or else [insane] or something
> worse... but let us not come up with any
> patronising nonsense about his being
> a great human teacher. He has not left
> that open to us. He did not intend to.'[3]

2. WHAT EVIDENCE IS THERE TO SUPPORT HIS CLAIMS?

- His teaching (Mark 12:31; Luke 6:31; Matthew 5:44)
- His life/works (John 2:1–11; 10:37–38)
- His character (Luke 23:34)
- His fulfilment of Old Testament prophecy
- His conquest of death

Evidence for the resurrection:

- **His absence from the tomb**
  - Theories:
    Jesus did not die (John 19:33–34)
    disciples stole the body
    authorities stole the body
    robbers stole the body (John 20:1–9)

- **His presence with the disciples**
  - Did they hallucinate?
  - Number of appearances over a six-week period
    11+ appearances
    500+ people
  - Nature of appearances (Luke 24:36–43)

- **Immediate effect**
  - Birth and growth of Christian church

- **Effect down the ages**
  - Experience of Christians down the ages
  - Over 2,300 million Christians in the world today

RECOMMENDED READING

Mere Christianity
C. S. Lewis

Jesus is
Judah Smith

....

....

....

....

....

....

....

....

....

....

....

....

....

....

....

Session 3

Why did Jesus die

Alpha

Why is the cross the symbol of Christianity?

'... the Son of God... loved me and gave himself for me'

(GALATIANS 2:20)

1. THE PROBLEM

'All have sinned and fall short of the glory of God.' (Romans 3:23).

- **Pollution** of sin (Mark 7:20–23)
- **Power** of sin (John 8:34)
- **Penalty** for sin (Romans 6:23)
- **Partition** of sin (Isaiah 59:2)

2. THE SOLUTION

- 'The self-substitution of God' (1 Peter 2:24)
- Agony of the cross (Isaiah 53:6)

3. THE RESULT

The cross shows:
- You are infinitely valuable to God
- Jesus is the supreme example of love (John 15:13)
- God is not aloof from suffering
- The powers of evil have been defeated: the resurrection wasn't the reversal of a defeat; it was the manifestation of a victory

- The **partition** has been removed (2 Corinthians 5:19)
  - Reconciliation with God and in other relationships

- The **penalty** has been paid
  - Justified ('Just-as-if-I'd never sinned')

- The **power** of sin has been broken
  - If the Son sets you free, you really will be free' (John 8:36, NLT)

- The **pollution** has been removed
  - '... the blood of Jesus cleanses us from all sin.' (1 John 1:7)
  - When you are forgiven, you want to forgive

RECOMMENDED READING

The Cross of Christ
John Stott

Searching Issues
Nicky Gumbel

Mud, Sweat and Tears
Bear Grylls

....
....
....
....
....
....
....
....
....
....
....
....

Session 4

How can I have faith

Alpha

'Those who become Christians become new persons. They are not the same anymore, for the old life is gone. A new life has begun!' (2 Corinthians 5:17, NLT)

A Christian is a *Christ*-ian: someone who follows and puts their faith in Jesus Christ.

How that happens varies enormously. For some there is a definite moment; for others it is a more gradual process.

- When you receive Christ, you become a child of God (John 1:12)
- God wants you to be sure of your faith

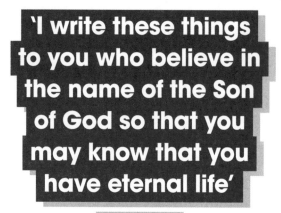

'I write these things to you who believe in the name of the Son of God so that you may know that you have eternal life'

(1 JOHN 5:13)

Faith is not a blind leap, but a step based on evidence.

1. THE WORD OF GOD

We must not only trust our feelings, which can be changeable and may even be deceptive at times, but instead rely on God's promises.

- '... faith comes from hearing, and hearing through the word of God.' (Romans 10:17)
- 'I will come in' (Revelation 3:20)
- 'I am with you always' (Matthew 28:20)
- 'I give them eternal life' (John 10:28)

2. THE WORK OF JESUS

You come exactly as you are. It's not about what you do or what you can achieve; it's about what has been done for you by Jesus on the cross.

- Free gift of God (Romans 6:23)
- It's free but not cheap: it cost Jesus his life
- We receive it through repentance (turning away from sin) and faith (trust)

3. THE WITNESS OF THE HOLY SPIRIT

When someone becomes a Christian, God comes to live inside them by his Holy Spirit (Romans 8:9).

- He transforms us from within
  - Our characters (Galatians 5:22–23)
  - Our relationships

- He brings a deep personal conviction that we are God's children
  - Faith to knowledge (Romans 8:15–16)

Here is a very simple prayer that you can pray to open the door of you heart to Jesus Christ and invite him to come into your life by his Spirit:

> Lord Jesus Christ,
> I am sorry for the things I have done wrong in my life (take a few moments to ask his forgiveness for anything particular that is on your conscience). Please forgive me. I now turn from everything that I know is wrong. Thank you that you died on the cross for me so that I could be forgiven and set free. Thank you that you offer me forgiveness and the gift of your Spirit. I now receive that gift. Please come into my life by your Holy Spirit to be with me forever.
> Thank you, Lord Jesus.
> Amen.

RECOMMENDED READING

The Reason for God
Tim Keller

Life Change
Mark Elsdon-Dew

Session 5

Why and
how do I
pray

Alpha

1. WHAT IS CHRISTIAN PRAYER?

Prayer is the most important activity of our lives.

'For through [Jesus] we both have access to the Father by one Spirit.' (Ephesians 2:18)

- **To the Father**
    - '... to your father' (Matthew 6:6)
    - '... in heaven' (v.9)
- **Through the Son**
    - 'I have called you friends' (John 15:15)
- **By the Spirit**
    - '... the Spirit helps us' (Romans 8:26)

2. WHY PRAY?

- Develops a relationship with God
- Rewards of prayer (Matthew 6:6)
    - Presence of God
    - Peace (Philippians 4:6–7)
    - Perspective
    - Power
- Results of prayer (Matthew 7:7–11)

'When I pray, coincidences happen, and when I don't, they don't'

**WILLIAM TEMPLE,
THE FORMER ARCHBISHOP OF CANTERBURY**

3. DOES GOD ALWAYS ANSWER PRAYER?

- **Yes** – you receive what you prayed for, sometimes immediately
- **No** – sometimes an obvious reason why not; other times we may not understand straight away why the answer is no
- **Wait** – for the right timing

4. HOW DO WE PRAY?

- **Thank you** – count your blessings, not your problems
- **Sorry** – confess your sins (John 13:6–10)
- **Please** – 'Give us today our daily bread' (Matthew 6:11): ask for anything you need

5. WHEN SHOULD WE PRAY?

- **Anywhere, anytime**
  - (Ephesians 6:18)
- **Alone (Matthew 6:6)**
  - Regular pattern
  - Best part of the day (Mark 1:35)
- **With others**
  - There's power in praying together
  - 'Where two or three are gathered in my name, there I am in their midst.' (Matthew 18:20)

Three simple tips:
- Keep it real
- Keep it simple
- Keep it going

RECOMMENDED READING

God on Mute, Pete Greig

How to Pray, Pete Greig

Prayer, Philip Yancey

Session 6

Why and how should I read the Bible

The Bible is the most...
- Popular
- Powerful
- Precious (Psalm 19:10)
... book in the world.

'People do not live on bread alone, but on every **word** that comes from the mouth of God' (Matthew 4:4).

1. BRINGING REVELATION – GOD HAS SPOKEN

- Bible – collection of books by 40+ authors over 1600 years
- Inspired: God-breathed

'All Scripture is inspired by God and is useful to teach us what is true; to make us realise what is wrong in our lives. It corrects us when we are wrong and teaches us to do what is right.' (2 Timothy 3:16).

But what about difficulties in the Bible?
- Jesus is the interpretive key
- It's authoritative (2 Timothy 3:16–17)
- Practical wisdom:
  - Guidelines for living
  - Guidance for good decisions

2. BUILDING RELATIONSHIP – GOD SPEAKS

The Bible is like a love letter from God:
- To those exploring faith (Romans 10:17; John 20:31)
- To those who are Christians
  - Become like Jesus (2 Corinthians 3:18)
  - Joy and peace in the midst of a storm (Psalm 23:5)
  - Guidance (Psalm 119:105)
  - Health/healing (Proverbs 4:20–22)
  - Defence against spiritual attack (Matthew 4:1–11)
  - Power (Hebrews 4:12)
  - Cleansing (John 15:3)

'Reading the Bible generates life. It produces change. It heals hurts. It builds character. It transforms circumstances. It imparts joy. It overcomes adversity. It defeats temptation. It infuses hope. It releases power. It cleanses the mind'

RICK WARREN

3. HOW DO WE HEAR GOD SPEAK THROUGH THE BIBLE?

- Make a plan
  - Find a time
  - Find a place ('a solitary place', Mark 1:35)

- Find a pattern
  - Ask God to speak:
    read a short passage
    Bible reading notes
    Bible in One Year app – bibleinoneyear.org

  - Ask yourself:
    what does it say to me?
    what does it mean to me?
    how does it apply to me?

- Respond in prayer
- Put it into practice (Matthew 7:24)

RECOMMENDED READING

Why Trust the Bible? Amy Orr-Ewing

30 Days, Nicky Gumbel

The Bible in One Year, Nicky Gumbel (Print and e-book)

Bible in One Year app with Nicky and Pippa Gumbel [iPhone/Android]

How does God guide us

Alpha

'For we are God's masterpiece. He has created us anew in Christ Jesus, so we can do the good things he planned for us long ago.' (Ephesians 2:10, NLT)

Why involve God in the decisions we make?

- God promises to guide us
  - (Psalm 32:8)
  - (John 10:3–4,27)

- God has a good plan for our lives
  - (Jeremiah 29:11)
  - (Romans 12:2)
  - (John 10:10,15)

How does God guide us?

1. COMMANDING SCRIPTURE

- General will
  - General instruction for marriage, work, money, children, elderly relatives (2 Timothy 3:16; Psalm 119:105, 130–133)

- Primary calling
  - To love God
  - To love others
  - To become like Jesus

2. COMPELLING SPIRIT

- God speaks as you pray (Acts 13:1–3)

- Strong desire to do something
  - 'God works in you to will and to act according to his good purpose' (Philippians 2:13)

- Sometimes he guides in more unusual ways
  - Prophecy, eg Agabus (Acts 11:27–28; 21:10–11)
  - Dreams (Matthew 1:20)
  - Visions/pictures (Acts 16:10)
  - Angels (Genesis 18; Matthew 2:19; Acts 12:7)
  - Audible voice (1 Samuel 3:4–14)

3. COUNSEL OF THE SAINTS

- '… the wise listen to advice' (Proverbs 12:15)

- 'Make plans by seeking advice' (Proverbs 20:18)

- Need for testing (1 John 4:1)
  - Is it in line with the Bible?
  - Is it loving? (1 John 4:16)
  - Is it strengthening, encouraging and comforting? (1 Corinthians 14:3)
  - Does it bring the peace of God? (Colossians 3:15)

Ultimately, we are responsible for our decisions, but it is a blessing to have others to talk to about the decisions we are making.

4. COMMON SENSE

- 'Reflect on what I am saying, for the Lord will give you insight into all this' (2 Timothy 2:7)

> **'God's promises of guidance were not given to save us the problem of thinking'**
>
> JOHN STOTT

5. CIRCUMSTANTIAL SIGNS

- 'And we know that in all things God works for the good of those who love him, who have been called according to his purpose.' (Romans 8:28)
- 'In your heart you plan your course, but the Lord determines your steps' (Proverbs 16:9; Psalm 37:5)
- Sometimes God closes doors (Acts 16:7)
- Sometimes God opens doors (1 Corinthians 16:9)
- Sometimes we need to persevere despite the circumstances and trust God
- Be patient
- We all make mistakes – God forgives (Joel 2:25)

RECOMMENDED READING

Chasing the Dragon
Jackie Pullinger

The Hiding Place
Corrie ten Boom

Who
is the Holy Spirit

For a long time in the church the person and work of the Holy Spirit has been:

- Ignored
  - Sometimes a greater concentration on the Father and the Son, but the Holy Spirit is biblical and is the third person of the trinity
- Misunderstood
  - 'Holy Ghost' sounds like an impersonal force. But the Holy Spirit is a person, not an 'it'
- Resisted
  - Fear of what might happen, but the Holy Spirit is gentle

1. HE WAS INVOLVED IN CREATION

- Bringing order out of chaos (Genesis 1:1–2)
- The Creator Spirit – giving life to mankind (Genesis 2:7)

2. HE CAME UPON PARTICULAR PEOPLE AT PARTICULAR TIMES FOR PARTICULAR TASKS

- Bezalel – for artistic work (Exodus 31:1–5)
- Gideon – for leadership (Judges 6:14–15,34)
- Samson – for strength and power (Judges 15:14)
- Isaiah – for prophecy (Isaiah 61:1–3)

3. HE WAS PROMISED BY THE FATHER

- The promise of a 'new thing'
  - 'I will put my Spirit in you' (Ezekiel 36:26–27)
  - 'I will remove your heart of stone and give you a heart of flesh' (Ezekiel 36:26–27)
  - 'I will pour out my Spirit on all people' (Joel 2:28–29)

However, the prophecies remained unfulfilled for at least 300 years.

With the coming of Jesus there is a great activity of the Spirit – not just for particular people at particular times but for everyone.

- Everyone surrounding the birth of Jesus is filled with the Holy Spirit:
  - Mary (Luke 1:35)
  - Elizabeth (Luke 1:41)
  - John the Baptist (Luke 1:15)

4. JOHN THE BAPTIST LINKS HIM WITH JESUS

'John answered them all, "I baptise you with water. But one more powerful than I will come, the thongs of whose sandals I am not worthy to untie. He will baptise you with the Holy Spirit and with fire."' (Luke 3:16)

- Jesus was filled with the Spirit
  - Jesus received power through the anointing of the Holy Spirit at his baptism (Luke 3:22; Luke 4:1,14,18)

5. JESUS PREDICTS HIS PRESENCE
(John 7:37–39)

However, he tells them to wait for the gift promised by the Father (Acts 1:4–5,8; Luke 24:49).

- At Pentecost the disciples were filled with the Spirit and received:
  - New languages (Acts 2:4–12)
  - New boldness (Acts 2:14)
  - New power (Acts 2:37–41)

We live in the age of the Spirit. God has promised to give his Spirit to every Christian (Acts 2:37–39)

'Whoever believes in me, as the Scripture has said, will have streams of living water flowing from within'

(JOHN 7:37–38)

RECOMMENDED READING

Come, Creator Spirit
Raniero Cantalamessa

....
....
....
....
....
....
....
....
....
....
....
....
....
....
....
....
....
....

Session 9

What
does the
Holy Spirit do

- New birth (John 3:3–8)
- Born into a family

1. SONS AND DAUGHTERS OF GOD

- Adoption (Romans 8:14–17)
  - Highest privilege (v.14)
  - Closest intimacy (v.15)
  - Deepest experience (v.16)

2. DEVELOPING THE RELATIONSHIP

'For through him we both have access to the Father by one Spirit.' (Ephesians 2:18)

- He helps us to pray (Romans 8:26)
- He enables us to understand God's word (Ephesians 1:17–18)

3. THE FAMILY LIKENESS

- He makes us more like Jesus (2 Corinthians 3:18)
- Fruit of the Spirit (Galatians 5:22–23)

4. UNITY IN THE FAMILY

- (Ephesians 4:3–6)

5. GIFTS FOR ALL THE CHILDREN

- The Holy Spirit gives everybody gifts for the common good (1 Corinthians 12:4–11)

6. A GROWING FAMILY

- The Spirit of God gives us power
  - To be witnesses for Christ (Acts 1:8)
  - For service (Acts 1:8)

'The Spirit and the bride say, "Come!" Let those who hear say, "Come!" Let those who are thirsty come; let all who wish take the free gift of the water of life.' (Revelation 22:17)

....

....

....

....

....

....

....

....

....

....

RECOMMENDED READING

The God Who Changes Lives Vol. 1, 2, 3 & 4
Ed. M. Elsdon-Dew

Session 10

How
can I be filled
with the
Holy Spirit

Alpha

What the Holy Spirit does and brings to our lives is all about love.

Every Christian has the Holy Spirit (Romans 8:9) but not every Christian is filled with the Spirit.

Five categories of people:

1. **Longing** (Pentecost – Acts 2:2–4)
2. **Receptive** (Samaria – Acts 8:14–23)
3. **Hostile** (Paul – Acts 8:1,3; 9:1–2)
4. **Uninformed** (Ephesus – Acts 19:1–6)
5. **Unlikely** (Gentiles – Acts 10:44–47)

What happened to Cornelius and his household when the Spirit came upon them? (Acts 10:44–46).

1. THEY EXPERIENCED THE LOVE OF GOD

'... the Holy Spirit came on all who heard the message. Then Peter said... 'they have received the Holy Spirit just as we have.'" (Acts 10:44–47)

- There were physical manifestations
- Everyone's experience is different
- What matters is God's love being poured out into your heart (Romans 5:5)
- Pursue the person, not the experience (Ephesians 3:14–19)

2. THEY EXPRESSED THEIR LOVE FOR GOD

'For they heard them... praising God' (Acts 10:46).

- Fear of emotion: emotion versus emotionalism
  - Emotion is an important part of faith and love for God
  - Express with our whole bodies: raised hands;
    a traditional form of prayer

3. THEY RECEIVED A NEW LOVE LANGUAGE

'For they heard them speaking in tongues' (Acts 10:46).

- Not all Christians speak in tongues
  - Not the mark of being a Christian
  - Not necessarily a mark of being filled with the Spirit
  - There are no first- or second-class Christians
  - It is not the most important gift

- What is the gift of tongues?
  - Human or angelic language (1 Corinthians 13:1)
  - A form of prayer (1 Corinthians 14:2)
  - Builds up the individual
  - Transcends the language barrier (1 Corinthians 14:14)
  - The speaker is in full control
  - Public use requires an interpretation

- Why is it helpful?
  - Worship (1 Corinthians 14:15)
  - Praying for oneself (1 Corinthians 14:2,4)
  - Praying for others

- Why ask for the gift of tongues?
  - Paul encourages its use (1 Corinthians 14:5,18,39)

What are the barriers to being filled with the Holy Spirit?
- Doubt: 'I don't think I will receive'
- Fear: 'What will happen to me'
- Inadequacy: 'I'm not good enough'

But Jesus says:

> **'... how much more will your Father in heaven give the Holy Spirit to those who ask him!'**
>
> **(LUKE 11:13)**

RECOMMENDED READING

The Mystery of Pentecost
Raniero Cantalamessa

Sober Intoxication of the Spirit: Filled with the Fullness of God
Raniero Cantalamessa

How can I make the most of the rest of my

life

Alpha

1. WHAT SHOULD WE DO?

- Break with the past
  - 'Do not conform any longer to the pattern of this world' (Romans 12:2)
  - 'Do not let the world around you squeeze you into its mould' (v.2, J. B. Phillips)[2]

- Make a new start
  - 'Let God transform you inwardly by a complete change' (v.2, GNT)

- God has treasures in store for us
  - Sincere love (v.9)
  - Enthusiasm in your relationship with God (Romans v.11)

2. HOW DO WE DO IT?

- 'Present your bodies…' (v.1)
  - Time
  - Priorities
  - Ambitions (Matthew 6:33)
  - Money
  - Ears
  - Eyes
  - Mouth
  - Hands
  - Sexuality

- '… as living sacrifices'
  - We will find freedom
  - There will be a cost
  - There will be challenges

3. WHY SHOULD WE DO IT?

- What God has done for us
  - '... in view of God's mercy' (v.1)

- What God has planned for our future
  - '... his good, pleasing and perfect will' (v.2)

RECOMMENDED READING

The Jesus Lifestyle
Nicky Gumbel

Life in Christ
Raniero Cantalamessa

How can I resist

evil

Alpha

Where does evil come from?

- Triple alliance:
  - World – the enemy around
  - Flesh – the enemy within
  - Devil – the enemy above

1. WHY SHOULD WE BELIEVE THAT THE DEVIL EXISTS?
(Romans 12:21)

- Scripture: The Bible presents a personal, spiritual being in active rebellion against God
  - Old Testament (Isaiah 14; Job 1; 1 Chronicles 21:1)
  - Jesus (Luke 10:17–20)
  - Peter (1 Peter 5:8–11)
  - Paul (Ephesians 6:11–12)

- Tradition: Christians down through the ages have believed

- Reason: It makes sense of the world we see around us
  - Why do bad things happen?

Avoid two extremes: Disbelief vs unhealthy, excessive interest

2. WHAT ARE THE DEVIL'S TACTICS?
(Genesis 3)

- The devil wants to destroy our lives (John 10:10)
    - Doubt (Genesis 3:1, Matthew 4:3)
    - Temptation (Genesis 2:16–17)
    - Deception (Genesis 3:4)
    - Condemnation

But, 'there is… no condemnation for those who are in Christ Jesus.' (Romans 8:1)

3. WHAT IS OUR POSITION?
(Colossians 1:13)

- We are transferred from the dominion of darkness to the kingdom of Jesus
- We experience God's love
- It's a process – we won't be complete until Jesus returns

4. HOW DO WE DEFEND OURSELVES?
(Ephesians 6)

'Be strong in the Lord… Put on the full armour of God so that you can take your stand against the devil's schemes.' (Ephesians 6:10–11)

1 Focus on Jesus – belt of truth (v.14)
- 'I am the truth.' (John 14:6)
- Authenticity, integrity, openness in your life

2 Keep your relationships right –
breastplate of righteousness (v.14)
- Keep short accounts with God
- Ask forgiveness from God and others

3 Get involved in service –
boots of the gospel of peace (v.15)
- The readiness to speak of Christ (Isaiah 52:7–10)

4 Trust God in difficult times –
shield of faith (v.16)
- The devil will challenge us with doubt, fear, anxiety, lust…
- Keep trusting; don't give up on your faith

5 Win the battle of the mind –
helmet of salvation (v.17)
- Salvation = freedom
- Protect your mind: temptation starts with a thought, which leads to action

6 Know your Bible –
sword of the Spirit (v.17)
- Soak yourself in the word of God
- The only offensive piece of armour (Hebrews 4:12)

5. HOW DO WE ATTACK?

- Prayer: 'Pray in the Spirit on all occasions...'
  (Ephesians 6:18)

- Action: 'Don't be overcome with evil, but overcome evil
  with good' (Romans 12:21)

RECOMMENDED READING

The Screwtape Letters
C. S. Lewis

Café Theology
Michael Lloyd

Session 13

Why
and
how
should I
tell

'Go and make disciples of all nations, baptising them in the name of the Father and of the Son and of the Holy Spirit, and teaching them to obey everything I have commanded you' (Matthew 28:18–20).

Why tell others?
- Jesus told us to
- For the needs of others – spiritual hunger in the world
- It's good news: 'gospel' = good news
- Two opposite dangers
  - Insensitivity
  - Fear

How do we tell others?

1. PRESENCE (Matthew 5:13-16)

- We are called to be salt and light (vv.13–14)
- When people know we are Christians, they watch our lives (v.16)

'You are the salt of the earth... You are the light of the world... let your light shine before others, that they may see your good deeds and praise your Father in heaven.' (Matthew 5:13–16)

2. PERSUASION (Matthew 5:13–16)

'Since… we know what it is to fear the Lord, we try to persuade people.' (2 Corinthians 5:11)

- Work out the answers to common questions
  - Eg: 'What about other religions?' and 'How can a God of love allow suffering?'
- Do it with gentleness and respect (1 Peter 3:15)

3. PROCLAMATION (John 1:39–46)

- We are not all called to be 'evangelists' but we are all called to be 'witnesses' (v.41)
- We can all say, 'Come and see'

4. POWER (1 Thessalonians 1:5)

- The love of God poured into our hearts by the Holy Spirit
- Healing

5. PRAYER (1 Thessalonians 1:5)

- For others
- For ourselves – to have boldness (Acts 4:29–31)

Don't give up – whenever you pass on the good news of Jesus, it has an effect. The gospel is the power of God (Mark 4:15–20).

RECOMMENDED READING

Lord... Help My Unbelief
John Young

Searching Issues
Nicky Gumbel

APPENDIX

Suggestions for preparing your story:

- **Keep it short**
  - Aim for three minutes – people switch off after that

- **Make it personal**
  - Don't preach – use 'I' or 'we' – not 'you'

- **Keep Christ central**
  - They need to follow him, not you

- **The format:**
  - A little of your former life
  - How you came into your relationship with Christ
  - Something of what it has meant since then

- **Write it out in full**
  - It's easier to edit your story when it's down on paper!

Session 14

**Does
God
heal
+oday**

Alpha

1. HEALING IN THE BIBLE

- Old Testament
  - 'I am the Lord who heals you' (Exodus 15:26)
  - The character of God – it's in his nature to heal
  - Examples of God healing (2 Kings 5; Isaiah 38–39)

- The ministry of Jesus
  - 'Jesus' means 'Saviour'
  - Greek sozo means 'I save', also 'I heal'
  - The healing miracles of Jesus form 25% of the Gospels
  - Jesus healed (Matthew 4:23)
      he gave his followers authority to heal (Luke 10:9, Acts)
      we see healing throughout church history
      he commissions us to pray for and heal the sick today

2. HEALING TODAY

- God heals explicably – through the medical profession
- God heals inexplicably and directly

'When we prayed for no one, no one was healed. Now we pray for lots of people and some are healed'

(JOHN WIMBER)

3. HOW DO WE HEAL?

- It's God who heals – not us

- Simplicity – pray as Jesus did with love and compassion (Matthew 9:36; Mark 1:41)

- Words of knowledge
  - Pictures
  - Sympathy pain
  - Impressions
  - Hear or see words

- Prayer – simple model
  - Where does it hurt?
  - Lay hands on the person
  - Ask the Holy Spirit to come
  - Ask how are they doing / if they can feel anything different
  - Sometimes you need to pray more than once

RECOMMENDED READING

Dirty Glory
Pete Greig

Power Evangelism
John Wimber

Session 15

What
about
the
church

What is the church?

- Popular misconceptions:
  - Church = services
  - Church = buildings

1. FRIENDS (John 15:15)

- Friends with Jesus
- Friends with one another (Hebrews 10:25)
- Greek word *koinonia* = fellowship

2. FAMILY (1 John 5:1)

- God as our Father (John 1:12)
- Brothers and sisters to each other (1 John 4:19 – 5:1)
- Importance of unity
- Jesus prayed '… that they may be one' (John 17:11)

Becoming a Christian involves:
- Something God does – he gives you the Holy Spirit
- Something you do – you repent and believe
- Something the church does – baptism

Baptism is the visible mark of being a member of the church.

Baptism signifies:
- Cleansing from sin (1 Corinthians 6:11)
- Dying and rising with Christ (Romans 6:3–5; Colossians 2:12)

3. HOME (Ephesians 2:19–22)

- Old Testament – physical temple was God's home
- New Testament – a building made up of people
  (Ephesians 2:21–22)
  - Jesus as the cornerstone (v.20)
  - Indwelt by God's Spirit (v.21) 'a holy temple'
  - A place where people are loved, accepted and
    welcomed home

4. JESUS (1 Corinthians 12:1–27)

- We are the body of Christ through whom the world will see
  Jesus (v.27)
- Universal church (Ephesians 3:10,21; 5:23,25)
  - Unity (John 17:20–21)
  - Diversity (Ephesians 4:7–11)
  - Mutual dependence (vv.14–26)

5. LOVE (Ephesians 5:25–27,32)

- Jesus loves the church; Jesus loves you (v.25)
- The church should be famous for its love

> **'You can do what I cannot do, I can do what you cannot do; together we can do great things'**

MOTHER TERESA

RECOMMENDED READING

Questions of Life
Nicky Gumbel

ENDNOTES

1. CS Lewis, The Weight of Glory (Zondervan: Michigan, 2001)

2. GOD IN THE DOCK by CS Lewis @ copyright CS Lewis Pte Ltd. 1970.

3. MERE CHRISTIANITY by C. S. Lewis copyright © C. S. Lewis Pte. Ltd. 1942. Extract reprinted by permission.

4. Reprinted by permission of HarperCollins Publishers Ltd. © (1973) (J. B. Phillips).